CW00330225

797,885 Books

are available to read at

www.ForgottenBooks.com

Forgotten Books' App
Available for mobile, tablet & eReader

ISBN 978-1-331-00193-5
PIBN 10132013

This book is a reproduction of an important historical work. Forgotten Books uses
state-of-the-art technology to digitally reconstruct the work, preserving the original format
whilst repairing imperfections present in the aged copy. In rare cases, an imperfection in
the original, such as a blemish or missing page, may be replicated in our edition. We do,
however, repair the vast majority of imperfections successfully; any imperfections that
remain are intentionally left to preserve the state of such historical works.

Forgotten Books is a registered trademark of FB &c Ltd.
Copyright © 2017 FB &c Ltd.
FB &c Ltd, Dalton House, 60 Windsor Avenue, London, SW19 2RR.
Company number 08720141. Registered in England and Wales.

For support please visit www.forgottenbooks.com

1 MONTH OF
FREE
READING

at

www.ForgottenBooks.com

By purchasing this book you are eligible for one month membership to ForgottenBooks.com, giving you unlimited access to our entire collection of over 700,000 titles via our web site and mobile apps.

To claim your free month visit:

www.forgottenbooks.com/free132013

* Offer is valid for 45 days from date of purchase. Terms and conditions apply.

English
Français
Deutsche
Italiano
Español
Português

www.forgottenbooks.com

Mythology Photography **Fiction**
Fishing Christianity **Art** Cooking
Essays Buddhism Freemasonry
Medicine **Biology** Music **Ancient
Egypt** Evolution Carpentry Physics
Dance Geology **Mathematics** Fitness
Shakespeare **Folklore** Yoga Marketing
Confidence Immortality Biographies
Poetry **Psychology** Witchcraft
Electronics Chemistry History **Law**
Accounting **Philosophy** Anthropology
Alchemy Drama Quantum Mechanics
Atheism Sexual Health **Ancient History**
Entrepreneurship Languages Sport
Paleontology Needlework Islam
Metaphysics Investment Archaeology
Parenting Statistics Criminology
Motivational

THE NEW SIN:
A Play in Three Acts, by
BASIL MACDONALD HASTINGS

LONDON : SIDGWICK & JACKSON, LTD.
3 ADAM STREET, W.C.   MCMXVI

Entered at the Library of Congress, Washington, U.S.A.

All rights reserved.

First Impression, February 1012.

Second   ,,   March 1916.

PERSONS CONCERNED

HILARY CUTTS

MAXIMILIAN CUTTS

JIM BENZIGER

WILL GRAIN, M.P.

DAVID LLEWELLYN DAVIDS, J.P., L.C.C., M.A.B.

STUART CAMPBELL

PEEL

SCENE

The Living Room of the West London Flat shared by Hilary Cutts and Jim Benziger

The interval between the first two Acts does not represent any lapse of time. That between Acts II. and III. represents a lapse of some months.

1012037

THE NEW SIN

A PLAY in three Acts by BASIL MACDONALD HASTINGS, first produced at the Royalty Theatre, London, W. (under the management of Messrs. J. E. VEDRENNE and DENNIS EADIE), on Tuesday the 20th of February 1912, with the following cast :—

Hilary Cutts . . .	Mr. ARTHUR WONTNER
Maximilian Cutts . .	Mr. O. P. HEGGIE
Jim Benziger . . .	Mr. MALCOLM CHERRY
D. L. Davids, J.P., L.C.C., M.A.B. . . .	Mr. A. G. POULTON
Will Grain, M.P. . .	Mr. GUY RATHBONE
Stuart Campbell . .	Mr. H. LANE-BAYLIFF
Peel	Mr. JAMES HEARN

The play produced by Mr. CLIFFORD BROOKE

I DEDICATE *The New Sin* to the dramatic critics in the hope that they will, at any rate, refrain from accusing me of committing an old sin.

THE AUTHOR

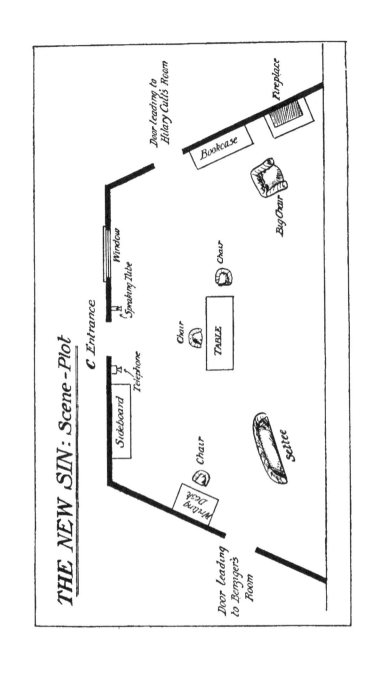

THE NEW SIN

ACT I

[JIM BENZIGER *enters from R. and goes to speaking tube by door C. He is a man of about thirty-two years of age, tall, slim, fastidiously dressed. He moves and speaks very quickly. He is wearing a flowered silk dressing-jacket with light grey trousers and slippers.*]

JIM [*at tube*]. That you, Peel? Porridge and cream, toast, the *Daily Mail,* a cup of strong coffee, my letters, a needle and thread and the *Times.* [*Puts tube to ear and then back to mouth.*] Mr. Cutts isn't up yet.

> [*Comes to table* C. *and removes decanter and glasses to sideboard. Alarum of clock in* HILARY CUTTS' *bedroom goes off,* L. *Muffled curses from* HILARY *off* L.

JIM. Hil, wake up. The cock has crowed, and Peel advises haddocks.

> [*Sound of boots being thrown at alarum clock off* L. *The first one misses. The second one finds its mark and the clock clatters to the floor.*

[*Enter* PEEL, *C., bearing tray on which are all* MR. BENZIGER'S *orders.* PEEL *is an old man, and his countenance is ascetic. He is really very feeble bodily, but he affects sprightliness in order to escape dismissal. He wears black-rimmed spectacles and is quite bald. Sometimes he looks like a librarian, sometimes like an alchemist, sometimes like a miser, but in his manner he is always at pains to admit that he is merely the flat porter.*

PEEL [*bringing tray to table, C.*]. The boy didn't leave the *Mail* this morning, sir, so I brought you the *Express* instead. It's just as expensive, sir, and so much more chatty, I think. Porridge and cream, toast, coffee [*ticking them off on his fingers*], the *Times,* and you'll find the needle and thread stuck in the loaf, sir. There were no letters for you this morning.

JIM [*who has snatched up the " Times " and extracted the Literary Supplement, pays no attention whatever to* PEEL, *but rushes to door of* HILARY'S *bedroom up L.*]. Hil, Hil! The *Times* has reviewed my novel. [*Indistinct swearing from* HILARY'S *room.* JIM *rattles the handle of the door.*] Let me in and I'll read it to you while you're dressing.

HILARY [*off*]. Go away, or I'll come out and strangle you.

JIM. Oh, all right—but I think you'd like to know that it says it's——

HILARY. Go away!

JIM. Oh, Hil, don't be so selfish. It says it's absorbing—absorbing, eh? And there's a bit about the heroine——

HILARY. Go away!

JIM. Oh, you're a bear!

> [*Goes towards table. As he does so door opens and* WILL GRAIN, M.P., *enters.*

JIM. Morning, Will. I say, the *Times* has reviewed my novel. I'll read it to you. Don't go, Peel. You may as well hear it. I'll lend you the book later on. Listen—

> " Mr. James Benziger has long been known to the public as the author of a number of successful melodramas, principally performed in the provinces "—

Not my fault. We broke the record for takings at Wigan. "Girl who ought to have told her parents."

> "It is a little startling to find his name on the cover of a really absorbing novel entitled *Nuts in May,* published by Messrs. Grin & Bearit. The story concerns one "—

But of course you don't want the plot.

> " The characters are all very pleasant people, and the heroine is just as charming as most girls .whose portraits appear on the cover are not. [*A little puzzled.*] But the chief charm of the book lies in its breezy air of optimism, and the author's healthy outlook on life."

Ha, ha! What do you think of that? [*laughing*].

"Healthy outlook on life!" [*Going to* HILARY's *door and knocking it.*]   Hil, ever noticed my healthy outlook on life?

[*A boot crashes against the door.*

PEEL.   Mr. Benziger, if I may interrupt you, the haddock is—er—hardening. *Rigor mortis*, sir. Returns after the escape of the heat. Not so pleasant to eat, but please yourself, of course, Mr. Benziger.

JIM.   You're quite right, Peel.   A man with a healthy outlook should eat his haddocks hot and read his *Times* cold.   Will, would you like a bit of the tail?

WILL.   Naw!   Ah'm a vegetarian.   [WILL GRAIN *is a North Countryman.   He is short and stout and has a splendidly rubicund countenance.   His voice booms.*]

JIM.   Of course, I forgot.   Peel, fetch Mr. Grain a nut [*indicating sideboard*].   When he has finished that, ask him to choose his own liqueur.

WILL.   You'll always laugh at me, Jim, but Ah've done well on nuts.   Whenever Ah sees a skiffy person, all spike an' tail, Ah says to myself, Ah says, ther' goes t' roast beef of Old England.   Folks that eat beef always grow up like skewers.

JIM [*excitedly*].   But the father and mother that bred you, Will, were not vegetarians.   You're a living example of a man unable to escape from the blessings of heredity.

PEEL [*noting the growing warmth of the conversation and anxious as ever to preserve peace*].   Well, Mr. Benziger, I'm sure I most heartily congratulate

,you on your success. I was certain the novel would bring you fame and fortune. You're a gentleman, sir, and the blood in you was bound to tell. A man's got to be well bred nowadays to get a novel published at 6s. with a picture cover. Before I came here, and many years ago it is, I was in service with a lord. He wasn't a real lord; that is to say, he hadn't a seat in the House. But he was the younger brother of a duke and always had vinegar with his hot fish. Well, he wrote a book and had it published. Beautifully bound it was too, but—sir! Well, there, we all know what a humbug Ruskin was. We all know what a humbug What's-is-name is now. But it simply sickened me to read what that man recommended as a rule of life. Art may be the end-all and the be-all of our earthly existence, but I couldn't bear reading homilies to that effect from a man who always helped himself to butter with his egg-spoon. But I mustn't interrupt your conversation, gentlemen.

[*Exit* PEEL, C.

JIM. There is something about Peel that makes me afraid of him. If he had the gift of expression, I think you would find that he knew something worth saying.

WILL [*who during* PEEL's *speech has taken* "*Daily News*" *from his overcoat pocket and is reading it*]. Well, Ah doan't know. Folks with the gift of expression are not generally given to thinkin' over much. Ah'm much more comfortable with a man that thinks a lot and says a little than with a dialectician who's slopping over with epigrams. [*Lowering his voice.*] Now, our friend Hilary Cutts here, he's got the gift of expression. Not so much in his talk, for sure, but in his pictures. Ah'm self-educated, but Ah can see the merit of his painting. One day he will be popular, and if he's lucky he'll be notorious. Ah don't think there's much depth in him, but he's ready, quick, nervous, sensuous, and sensitive. You know Ah'm fond of him. We three men have no secrets, so Ah'm going to ask you a straight question, Jim. Isn't he drinking too much?

JIM. Yes. He's hard up, as stony as a man can be. I've lent him all I can afford. There was a devil of a debauch here last night.

WILL. Why is it? He earns a decentish income. Those trashy things he does for the illustrated papers are well paid for, and he does a lot of them.

JIM. Well, I can't explain it, of course. But I do know that whenever he gets a cheque I find the counterfoils of postal orders about the flat.

WILL. Ah—for sure. Then he's posting the best part of his money away. Who to? A woman.

JIM. My dear, stupid old Will. Why do you always associate money with women?

WILL. Ah doan't know. It seems natural.

JIM. Besides, Hil, I know—merely from observation, mind you—doesn't care a straw about women. In fact, they seem to irritate him. He is always uncomfortable in their presence.

WILL. Then it's a book-maker.

JIM.   He hardly knows the difference between a
colt and a filly.

WILL.   Those are just the folk that bet.

JIM.   Well, he's not one of them.   I should know
about it if he gambled.   He is keeping something
from us that he is ashamed of, and betting is a positively virtuous hobby—as things go nowadays.

WILL.   Then he's supporting his parents.

JIM.   Who are both dead.   I know that much,
but Hilary's family history is not a subject that he
has ever talked much about.

WILL.   Meanwhile, he's drinking himself to death.

JIM.   Rubbish [*rising from table and going down
to* WILL].   You're an incorrigible old—well, an incorrigible old Labour Member.   Nearly everything
you say is an exaggeration.   And you make yourself so unhappy by exaggerating, and every one else
unhappy too.   I suppose you know your business.
You were elected to Parliament very largely by the
votes of ignorant people.   I don't say they're wrong,
mind.   I simply say they are ignorant.   Exaggeration, big talk of any description hypnotises the
uneducated.   Therefore, you and the fellow-members
of your party are necessarily intemperate in your
speech.   I talk a good deal, I admit—almost every
dramatist does—but I could write a letter on a
visiting-card, while you would wish a man a Happy
Christmas on a double-crown poster.   To say Hilary
is drinking himself to death because he occasionally
gets decently drunk is as bad as to say that a man
is eating himself to death because he occasionally

sleeps after his luncheon.   You're a teetotaler because
you prefer it.   A glass of whisky would make you
sick.   Well, do you know that the avoidance of
alcohol in your case makes you a disgusting hedonist ?
You ought to get drunk occasionally—for your sins,
just as the hard drinker occasionally gives up alcohol
—for his.

WILL.   That's silly.   Ah tell you Ah had the vice
as a very young man, and Ah gave it up.

JIM.   It gave you up.   A temptation has got a
soul.   A temptation is a very fastidious ism.   You
gave way too easily, too abjectly, and the temptation
deserted you as an unworthy opponent.   If a very
bad boxer challenges again and again for a championship, and is constantly beaten, the time comes when
he can't get another match with the champion.   He
doesn't want to give up trying for the championship,
but the champion ignores his impudent claims.   You
don't drink alcohol because it has given you a sound
thrashing, and won't be bothered with you any more.

WILL.   Well, of all the damned impudence !

> [*Enter* HILARY CUTTS *from L.   He is
> in his trousers and shirt.   He
> wears a belt instead of braces.
> He is a clean-shaven, heavily
> built man of about* 35.   *There is
> a suggestion of dissipation about
> his eyes.*

HILARY.   Got a stud, Jim ?

JIM.   Yes ; you'll find one in——

HILARY. [*interrupting him*].   Hello, Will ! I didn't

know you were here. How goes the Public Health Bill? [*He speaks very heartily.*]

WILL. Ah, so, so, Hilary.

HILARY. Where did you say that stud was, Jim?

JIM. You'll find it in a small, silver-coloured box, labelled "Odds and Ends," at the left corner of the shelf on my dressing-table, and, for the sake of the Prophets, don't upset everything.

HILARY. Delicate Jim! Delicate Jim! You ought to have been a Civil Service clerk on £200 per annum—with notepaper. Everything in its place except yourself when the Chief's away. [*Walking out R.*] I don't believe there's another man from here to Buckingham Street who keeps a reserve stud on the premises.

[*Off.*

JIM. Well, how does he look for a man who is drinking himself to death?

WILL [*surlily*]. The dead are often healthier to look at than the living.

JIM. Oh, you give me the miserables. [*Crash from off R., where* HILARY *has upset box off dressing-table.*] What the devil is he up to?

[*Rushes off R.* WILL *laughs.* HILARY *is
        thrust out of* JIM's *room by the
        shoulders.*

HILARY. Well, I'm sure I'm very sorry; but I got the stud, and I would certainly have cleared up the foundry if you had let me. [*Turning to* WILL.] Impudence on its dignity! Well, Will, you know I'm really anxious to hear how this precious Bill of

B

yours is going. It ought to make you famous. Then an Under-Secretaryship will come, then a Cabinet post. Why, we may even see you in the House of Lords.

WILL.   Not me, Hil. Ah'm a man of the people, and to the people Ah'm going to stick.

HILARY.   Rather a quixotic notion. [*Moving off to his room.*] The tram fare from Battersea is just the same to both Houses.

[*Exit L.*

JIM [*entering from R.*]. Hil is the most careless scamp I ever met. As a politician he'd mislay his views.

HILARY [*re-entering from L.*].   Ah, Jim, I've found my stud. Could you—could you spare me a collar, do you think?

JIM [*snappishly*].   Haven't you got one left?

HILARY.   They're at the laundry, Jim, and—well, the laundry happens to belong to a firm with an unreasonable aversion to post-dated cheques.

JIM.   Oh, that's the way, is it? All right. [HILARY *moves across as if to enter* JIM's *room again.*] No, you don't. I'll get the collar, thank you, Hil.

HILARY.   Very nice of you, Jim. Choose something quiet, will you?

[*Exit* JIM, *R.*

WILL.   You do lead poor old Jim a deuce of a dance.

HILARY.   A polka, Will, merely a polka. The first dance we all learn as children. "My mother said—I never should—do anything—if another chap would."

WILL.   How goes the world of Art?

HILARY.   Splendidly, Will. I have had a picture

accepted by the Academy and a painting accepted by the Salon.

JIM [*re-entering from R., and bringing with him a pair of trousers, buttons, and the collar*]. Here's your collar. And mind, when you have finished with it, give it to me, not to your laundry.

HILARY [*bowing low*]. Benefactor! I shall remember!

[*Exit L. buttoning on collar.*

WILL. Is he going to have any breakfast?

JIM [*who has taken needle and thread from loaf, sits R. and sews buttons on trousers*]. Well, judging from what remains of the decanter, I shouldn't say this was one of his breakfast mornings.

[*Enter HILARY from L., pulling a woollen sweater over his head.*

JIM. Going to have any breakfast, Hil?

HILARY [*with his head still in the sweater*]. Of course I am.

JIM. Peel advises haddocks.

HILARY. Well, I don't think anything else would blend very well with the aroma of the room at present. [*Goes to tube and blows down.*] Breakfast! [*Coming down C.*] Yes, Will, the world of Art is quite nice to live in just now.

WILL. Then you're making money.

HILARY. Well, no. I'm happy because I'm doing good work, and that is rarely paid for. The demand for drawings in the illustrated papers is decreasing. Editors prefer smoky photographs. You can't blame them. They're cheaper. Then so much

space has to be given to portraits — portraits of
celebrities and June brides—you know the sort of
thing.   The "photocracy" I believe they call them.

[*Enter* PEEL *bearing breakfast tray, on
which is a haddock, coffee, bread
and butter, and a packet of letters.*

PEEL.   Your breakfast, Mr. Cutts.   It's a nice
haddock, straight from Loch Lomond, I'm told.
Ah, these Scotchmen—[*laying table*]—they know
what's good, sir.   I'm sure if my parents could have
afforded to have brought me up on porridge and haddocks, I could have sub-edited any paper in London.

HILARY [*abstractedly.   He has been examining the
envelopes of the letters.*]   Yes, yes, Peel.   Er—clean
my boots.

PEEL [*moving towards door L.*].   Certainly, sir.
There's one little matter I must mention, rather an
unpleasant matter, sir.   You know the gentleman
who occupies the flat below this.

JIM.   Fat?   Sandy?   Spats?   Diamonds?   Gold
pince-nez?   General expression like a conscience-
stricken company promoter?

PEEL.   He's a member of the London County
Council, and, I believe, of the Asylums Board, not
to mention being a J.P.

WILL.   What's his name?

PEEL.   David Llewellyn Davids, sir.   From
Cheshire.

WILL.   Ah know him.   Damned ignorant brute.
Ah've interviewed him in connection with my bill.
He knows no more about lunatics or Local Govern-

ment than—this newspaper. [*Waving his news-paper.*]

JIM. Draper or haberdasher, isn't he?

WILL. Aye, and one of the worst sweaters in London.

PEEL. He doesn't live here regularly, of course. Indeed, I've heard him call it his *pied à terre*.

WILL. What's that mean?

PEEL [*airily*]. French, sir, French. It might mean anything.

WILL. Who's that woman down there?

PEEL. Why, who but Mrs. Davids, Mr. Grain.

[WILL *and* JIM *chuckle.*

JIM. Ah, Peel, the world is full of such Mrs. Davids.

HILARY [*who has been reading his letters*]. Now, no scandal. Get to the point, Peel. Why do you mention his name?

PEEL. Well, sir, I believe it is true that there was rather a boisterous party here last night.

HILARY. Yes. Jim and I and another chap got drunk. One of the features of the evening was a Wagnerian tone poem played on three tin trunks with a poker, tongs, and shovel. There was also some comic singing. Jim insisted on inflicting upon us a plaintive ditty called "Playing the game in the West." He liked his version so much that he kept on singing it for three-quarters of an hour. Then he fell off his chair and started pulling up the boards of the floor, seeking, as he said, for hidden treasure.

PEEL. Yes, sir. A great deal of plaster fell in the room below, sir.

HILARY. I'm not surprised. Mr. Benziger will, of course, apologise to Mr. Davids.

JIM. I'll see him damned first. But you'll have to apologise, Hil.

HILARY. What did I do?

JIM [*to* PEEL]. Do they complain of any—dampness downstairs?

PEEL. They say the ceiling of the bedroom is nearly melted away. It dripped from 1-30 till 2-15 this morning.

HILARY. Ah, there must have been a storm last night.

JIM. Soon after one o'clock this morning, Hil, you were so full of liquor that you suddenly felt a maudlin sympathy, so you said, for the poor souls who were thirsting in Hell. So for the next hour you let the bathroom taps run wild over the floor; a foolish proceeding, because the water does not seem to have got any farther than the Davids' flat.

HILARY. Well, what is the upshot, Peel?

PEEL. Simply that you may expect a visit from Mr. Davids this morning. He is—er—exceedingly exasperated.

HILARY. Is that all? We shall probably be out, but he's welcome. Don't forget those boots.

[*Exit* PEEL, *L.*

[HILARY *gets sheet of notepaper from desk R., and returns to table C.*

WILL. Well, Ah'm very surprised at both of you.

It'll drag you down, this drink. You can't do good work if you drug your brains, for sure.

JIM. But Hilary has been doing good work, and he's hard up. I've been doing bad work, and the public are acclaiming me nightly.

WILL. Bah! Your plays are just a prostitution.

JIM. I'm not proud of them, but I'm proud of the fact that I can sell them.

[*Re-enter* PEEL *from L. with boots.*

HILARY [*who has been scribbling on the sheet of notepaper, and paying no attention to the conversation*] Peel, I am going to commit suicide.

PEEL. Yes, sir. Didn't you like the haddock, sir?

HILARY. I have made a will. There it is, on half a sheet of notepaper. Mr. Grain will witness it, and I want you to witness it also.

PEEL. Certainly, sir. Have you made me an executor, sir?

HILARY. No, Peel; you are merely a witness.

PEEL. I don't quite like that, sir. Witnesses always die, I've noticed, from reading the papers. Executors generally live.

JIM. Don't you want to die, Peel? You're old enough.

PEEL. Well, if I may take you gentlemen into my confidence, I should like to die; but I know it would annoy Mrs. Parsons exceedingly. One of the cats passed away on Tuesday—the grey one, gentlemen, with the ultramarine eyes—and she's been so upset and everybody in the household has suffered.

HILARY. Sign, Peel. The cat or I. You or the

cat.   What's the odds?   [PEEL *takes pen, and writes his name neatly with a flourish.*]   There are tears for a man, tears for a dumb animal, and all of it unnecessary.   It's the comedy of life.   You don't read Pascal, do you, Peel?   Begin [*indicating bookshelf*]. Third shelf from the bottom, fifth volume from the left.

> [PEEL *crosses to bookshelf and takes down the volume, handling it very gingerly.   He pushes his spectacles up to his forehead, and looks into the book with his eyes close to the page.* HILARY *picks up the will, glances at the signature, and laughs.*

WILL.   What's the joke, Hil?

> [HILARY *passes paper to* WILL, *who looks at it and laughs.* JIM *holds out his hand for it, and* WILL *throws it to him.* JIM *examines it and laughs. All are laughing together.*

WILL.   Where did you get this, Peel?

PEEL [*who is reading*].   I beg your pardon, sir.

JIM.   How did you come to be called this?

PEEL [*smiling*].   Ah!   My Christian names, gentlemen.   Yes, my names are Pontius Pilate Peel.   It happened this way [*resuming spectacles*].   My father, you see, was an irreligious man.   He never troubled to have us christened, and one day a visiting cleric discovered the unsavoury fact.   I was taken to church for the first time at the age of nine.   My

father didn't much care about the business, but he
consented in the end, and decided to call me
Machiavelli. The curate absolutely declined to give
me that name, and suggested something scriptural.
So my father decided on Pontius Pilate because, as
he said, I was such a dirty little beggar, and had
only once been known to wash my hands. [*They
laugh.*] Yes, gentlemen, he was a heathen; but
what a sense of humour! If I may, sir, I will take
this volume away with me.

HILARY. By all means, Peel.

PEEL. I will return it to-morrow, but I will ask
you to excuse me now. Number 14 is having in coal
at twelve o'clock, and there's a hole in Number 8's
reserve dustbin that I must patch up before dinner.
So you'll excuse me, and thank you, gentlemen.

[*Exit with boots and book.*

JIM. Why this sudden outburst of generosity,
Hil? [*waving the will*] I don't want you to die, and
I certainly don't want your property.

HILARY. Well, I'm leaving you the chattels because
you will probably be sentimental enough to pay my
funeral expenses.

WILL [*growling from behind his paper*]. Ah, cut
that out. It isn't decent—all this flippant talk
about death and suicide.

JIM. Decency, my dear Will, is the pet shibboleth
of the ignorant—and the *Spectator*.

HILARY. The indecency doesn't concern me. I'm
looking forward to it, positively looking forward
to it.

WILL. See here, Hil, Ah've never been able to tell whether you're serious or not, but if there is anything behind all this talk, why not let your friends into the secret?

HILARY [*still fingering the letters*]. Certainly. I am very shortly going to take my life—very shortly —but, of course, don't leave any sooner than you want to.

JIM. I shouldn't do it in any way likely to cause pain to your relations. Make it look as if it were an accident.

HILARY. Very thoughtful of you, Jim.

JIM. Not at all. Are you insured?

HILARY. Good Heavens, no! You know I live absolutely from hand to mouth. I owe two months' rent for my share of this flat.

JIM. Then you are not living from hand to mouth. Blessed are they that owe, for they invariably live in luxury. But don't change the subject. How will you do it?

HILARY. I might not be able to pluck up courage enough to execute myself. Couldn't you murder me?

JIM [*jumping up excitedly*]. By Jove, Hil, what a splendid notion!

> [WILL, *with an exclamation of disgust, rises and goes up to door C., picking up his hat.*

HILARY. Don't go, Will [*bringing him down to chair again*]. You may be able to help me. But let me settle this point with Jim first. [*To* JIM.] If

I were to consent to your murdering me, should I be doing you a good turn?

JIM. Tremendous. In the first place, I don't think a man has ever consented to be murdered before in real life. It would be a new thing to do. That makes it worth while.

HILARY. But you wouldn't run the risk of being hanged, Jim, merely for the sake of testing a new sensation.

JIM. I should run no risk, as I will willingly explain to you. But it's not only for the sake of doing something novel that I am so glad of the opportunity. You know that I am a playwright— a melodramatist. Every play that I have written, or, I should say, every play of mine that has drawn royalties, contains at least two murders. I have never committed a murder. I have never seen one. Look what a tremendous advantage it would be to me to have experienced the sensation of blowing another man's brains out. I could write a murder scene that would paralyse humanity. I should—er —make more money.

HILARY. You needn't be so damned enthusiastic about it.

JIM. I can't help it. It's the chance of a lifetime.

HILARY. It would serve you right if you were afterwards hanged for it.

JIM. Impossible. You have a revolver? Of course. And cartridges? Of course. You give me the weapon. I shoot you close to the temple and

kill you. I rouse the house after placing the revolver in your hand. The police find you with
a letter in your pocket admitting your intentions.
I swear that I witnessed the deed, and was too late
to prevent it. *Voilà tout!*

> [HILARY *coughs, walks to the fireplace
> and fills his pipe from the jar.*

HILARY. You're a selfish devil, Jim.

JIM. Not at all. If you wish to live I am the
last to interfere. If you wish to die, why not employ
me to effect what you would never have the courage
to do yourself?

HILARY. Hang your reasoning. If I've got to
die, I'll stage-manage the business myself. I'm not
particularly squeamish, but I don't like the idea of
selling my body before it's cold. That's what it
comes to.

JIM. Pah! You're sentimental.

HILARY. Sentimental! What a charge! Do
either of you men know who my father was?

JIM. No. [WILL *shakes his head.*]

HILARY. You don't! [*Down C.*] Pull up your
trousers. [*Both stare at him in amazement.*] Pull
them up, I tell you. [*They do so with muttered
comments.*] Higher! [*They pull them almost to the
knee, revealing sock-suspenders.* JIM'S *socks are very
gay,* WILL'S *very homely.*] I thought so! [*pointing
dramatically at their suspenders.*] "Cutts' Unslippable Sock-suspender." The invention that made
my father famous—brought him a fortune and a
knighthood. Ever since 1875 my father has had his

grip on the calves of the aristocracy. True, he is now dead, but his handiwork reposes at this moment under every well-cut trouser in the civilised globe.

WILL. So you're the son of Sir Nathaniel Cutts. [HILARY *nods*.]

JIM. Left rather a peculiar will, didn't he? [HILARY *nods*.] Odd that I should never have connected you with him. But you have always been such a secretive beggar about your family.

HILARY. I have good reason. But you shall hear something of them now. Nathaniel Cutts, my father, married one of his shop assistants. He acquired great wealth from his haberdashery business, and more particularly from the exploitation of the Unslippable Sock-suspender. He eagerly spent his thousands on the education of his children, myself, Ian, Millicent, Angus, Evelyn, Roy, Stephanie, Marcus, Miriam, Maximilian, Ellaline, and Cyril. My mother named us all. We boys went to a famous public school, and most of us afterwards to universities; the girls were over-educated by sentimental professors at home. Unfortunately, the family turned out badly. I, the eldest, proved a shocking scapegrace, and nearly broke my father's heart. I was forbidden the privilege of crossing the family threshold at the age of twenty-two. My brothers and sisters were really no better. They were even less capable than I; but they adroitly managed to retain a semblance of the parental favour. My mother was the first to die, followed by my father six months later. I was then thirty-three.

The will, as you say, Jim, was a remarkable document. It decreed that the money was to be divided equally among the children, with the exception of me. I was to have absolutely nothing. It seems a cruel arrangement, but there were good reasons for the old man's bitterness.

WILL [bluntly]. What were they?

HILARY. I don't care about repeating a very unpleasant story. Not only was I to derive no benefit from my father's estate, but during my lifetime the same disability attached to my brothers and sisters. The old man had cunningly guessed that cutting me out of his will would by no means prevent me from living comfortably on my brothers' and sisters' money. He knew that I was the idol of the family, and that his wishes as to the disposal of the money would certainly be thwarted. He therefore decided on this very eccentric scheme. The whole of his property was to be capitalised, and the interest was to be allowed to accumulate until such time as I chose to die. Then, and not till then, my eleven brothers and sisters would have his fortune.

JIM. The hard-hearted old skinflint.

WILL. He should have given his money to charity sooner than do that.

HILARY. When the terms of the will were known, I promptly became very unpopular with my brothers and sisters. My continued existence was irksome to them. The youngest, Cyril, had just turned nineteen, so that all were of an age at which work is endurable. To their credit, I must say that they all made an attempt to earn a living. There was, indeed, nothing else for them to do.

WILL. Why didn't they borrow on the reversion?

HILARY. There was a clause in the will forbidding anticipation.

WILL. H'm. That settles it.

HILARY. Of all the twelve I was the most successful. I alone had any sort of individuality. I did fairly well as a designer of stained-glass windows, and afterwards as a full-fledged artist. But my tastes were expensive. I borrowed more than I made. I gave away more than I borrowed.

One by one my brothers and sisters found me out. Each one of them begged of me. They imagined I made more than was actually the case. The whole eleven were failures—the girls because they were plain, and the boys because they were too ornamental. Hardly a day passes on which I do not receive a despairing letter from at least one of them. Their appeals to me, the cause of all their troubles, worry me to distraction. I like them all. I know that it is not their fault that they are failures, and I am intensely conscious of the fact that only my physical being stands between them and happiness.

WILL. And that's the reason why you contemplate suicide?

HILARY. It is. I can't stand it any longer. This morning there are letters from six—actually six of them. They're tragic, awful letters! They'd bring tears to the eyes of a statue.

WILL.   Can't you get this will set aside?

HILARY.   No.   Similar wills have been made before on at least two occasions.   Every legal weapon was employed to revoke them, but the wills stood.   Even if there were a chance, where is the money to come from for the legal expenses?

JIM.   You seem to have got more than your fair share of misery, Hil.

HILARY.   It's worse for them.   Listen to this [*opening a letter*]—" I only want three-and-six.   It will get me a bed and food for the week, and I've a promise of work on Monday.   If I don't get the money to sleep indoors I'll get my clothes worse, and they're very bad now.   A clerk has got to dress decently.   I met Miriam accidentally yesterday. She's living with Ella.   Ella's very ill, she told me, but Miriam is getting fourteen shillings at a tea-shop.   She wanted to give me sixpence, but I'm damned if I'd take it from her.   Send me the money if you can, old man.   I don't want to shame you by calling on you as I am.—Your brother,   ROY.

" *P.S.*—Oh, my God, what wouldn't I give to be able to shave every day."

They're all like that.   Ella, it seems, is dying from consumption.   And there's one here from another sister.   She's hard up, she says.   She's very hard up.   She says—she says—there's scent on the paper.   She says — she writes from 17A Apollo Mansions, Shaftesbury Avenue.   She wants money

to keep her — and something else — alive.   She
doesn't know who——

> [*Crushes the letters up and throws them
> in the fire, remaining at fireplace,
> with his head buried in his arms.*

WILL.   It's very dreadful for you, Hil, but Ah
don't see yet why you should sacrifice yourself foɪ
them.   How much money will they get each when
you die ?

HILARY.   Ten thousand pounds.

WILL.   Ten thousand pounds !

JIM.   Really, as much as that !

HILARY.   It might be more.   It increases every
moment of the day.

WILL.   And you propose to kill yourself—the only
member of the family likely to be any good in the
world—just for the sake of putting all that money
into the hands of people who obviously could only
go to the devil on it.   What good is the money
going to do to them or the world when you
release it ?

HILARY.   Argued like a Socialist, Will.   Do you
think I don't realise how illogical such a step would
be ?   But that doesn't save me from taking it.
You fellows want us to accept Government by brain.
Well and good.   But you must first cut out our
hearts.   Goodness knows I don't want brothers and
sisters to love but I've got 'em, and by a law of
nature I must love 'em.   If I were a reasonable
man I should ignore 'em, let 'em go to the devil.
But I'm not reasonable.   A blood tie stifles reason.

You Socialists are transcendently irrational because
you expect humanity to be rational. We are not
rational. We never shall be. The old saying,
" Blood is thicker thàn water " simply means
" Humanity is too human to be humane." Suppose
you have a deformed child. You ought to destroy
it. But if the State let you, you wouldn't do it.
You preach—the whole jim bang lot of you—a
code which you yourselves could never practise.

WILL. Ah don't know that Ah suggested you
should send them to the devil. Ah certainly didn't
intend to. What Ah say is that a man's life belongs
to the nation and to Heaven and you're——

JIM. Spare us that, Will.

WILL. Oh, Ah can see my advice isn't wanted,
but——

HILARY. Nonsense, Will, don't let's quarrel.

WILL. Ah'm not going to quarrel, but Ah say
that any man who encourages you to take that
cowardly way out of trouble is a bad friend.

HILARY. Will, do you realise the state of affairs
those letters reveal? My younger brothers, my
younger sisters, starving. Poor bodies, poor brains,
but my flesh and blood. They've worked, they've
striven, but the world's been too much for them.
They weren't born for or to expect hard fighting.
They're all gone, or going under. It's awful, awful,
awful. The little sisters, Jim, I used to escort to
parties. Pretty, pink little kids they were then, in
their little lace frocks and silk stockings, coloured
ribbons, and long loose hair. Little dears. Little

dears. Excuse me sniffling. Then the boys, tough little chaps, they seemed once. They worshipped me, the oldest, the biggest, the strongest. They fagged for me, swore by me, lied for me, and yes—God bless 'em—to me. Jim, I can't let them go right under. I didn't mind their having troubles. When they grew older and more smug, I lost a lot of my love for 'em. But at a time like this it comes back—the old feeling. Blood, blood, blood—it rules the will, the brain. They'll be no good to any one when they get the money. I'm some good as I am. My work's good. I might yet produce something that the world would be glad of, pleased always to remember. They never will. Yet I must die. It's my duty. I'm sinning every moment I live. To live—to sin! Is that a paradox? It's a new sin, Jim. To sin by living! It is wrong of me not to destroy myself. But it's hard, hard, damned hard.

> [JIM *rises and lays his hand on* HILARY's
> *shoulder. Then exit R.*

WILL. Ah'm real sorry for you, Hil, and Ah'm not going to say any more to influence you one way or the other. It's a job only one man can tackle and you're the only one that's got the hang of it. But if you want to end your life, don't ever be such a fool as to strike the blow yourself.

HILARY. You mean I ought to close with Jim's interesting offer.

WILL. No, no, nothing of the sort. Jim's a humbug.

HILARY. Then what on earth do you mean?

WILL. Hil, there are many things a man can do if he is willing to surrender his life. A human life can buy great benefits for humanity.

HILARY. Do, do explain, Will.

WILL. Supposing you were to kill some one, Hil. Well, you would be hanged. Unpleasant, but so is shooting, poisoning, or drowning oneself. Suppose the man you selected to kill were some evil-living brute in high places, some scourge of humanity that the law is powerless to touch. Then you would not have sacrificed your life entirely in vain. Ah'm not an anarchist. Ah'm no enemy of Kings—God help them in these days—but Ah've got the lust for the blood of several men Ah might name. Wouldn't it be easy to find one? Some slave-driving Christian for example. Some wealthy beast who buys the chastity of children, some money-mad brute that sweats our youth and pitches the middle-aged into the street. There's plenty of them. The wrongs of the proletariat——

[*Enter* JIM *dressed for the street, from R.*

JIM. Ah, Will, practising for Hyde Park? I'm going to the Post Office. I'll go down to the bus with you.

[*Up to door C.*

WILL [*surlily*]. All right, Jim.

JIM. I shall be back in a few minutes, Hil. We'll talk it over a little more calmly then. Don't listen to old Will. I believe at heart he disapproves of the spirit of the Crucifixion.

[*Exit C.*

WILL [*goes after* JIM, *turns back and comes down to* HIL]. Look here, Hil, Ah'm a Member of Parliament. You can get a will like this set aside by an Act of Parliament. Ah know that much. My brother's chairman of the Labour Party. Ah'll ask him what he can do. This Government can do nothing without our votes. We've got them under our thumbs. Ah'll get him to force 'em to put a bill through. Ah'll make it right yet, Hil. Ah'll make it right.

[*Exit C.*

HILARY [*laughing cynically*]. Dear old Will! [*He goes to door C., then down to table C., then back to window L.C., and putting his head out watches his departing friends. He shuts the window and crosses R.C., to desk. He takes out of a drawer a parcel containing revolver and cartridges and proceeds to load the weapon.*] It's a fascinating thing, this. Made to kill men. Never be used again Locked up in a glass case in Scotland Yard, or possibly purchased by an amateur criminologist. What was Will's idea? Kill some one else and get hanged for it. Not a bad notion. Difficult to work up any indignation, though, against the people Will mentioned. He suggested a slave-driving Christian, I think, or a perverter of youthful morals, or—let me see—what was the other type?

[*Enter* PEEL, *C.*

PEEL. Mr. David Llewellyn Davids!

[*Enter* MR. DAVIDS, *C., very pompously,* HILARY *stands with his back to*

the audience, facing DAVIDS, *hold-*
ing the revolver behind his back.
[MR. DAVIDS *is slightly corpulent and*
of medium height. His hair is
sandy and is dressed oilily and
flamboyantly like a cheap barber's.
He wears spats, diamonds, and gold
pince-nez. His silk hat gleams
brightly, and his grey frock suit
outlines his fat, but not, therefore,
ungraceful figure.

CURTAIN

ACT II

[*Scene as at the conclusion of the first Act.* PEEL *has gone, but* DAVIDS *and* HILARY *are facing each other as before, the latter still holding the revolver behind his back.*]

HILARY [*gradually slipping revolver into his pocket so that* DAVIDS *does not notice it*]. Good morning. I suppose you want to know the why and the wherefore of the row up here last night.

DAVIDS [*whose voice is thick, and has an improved Cockney twang*]. Last night and this morning.

HILARY. Take a chair. [DAVIDS *sits on chair back of table C.*] We, of course, owe you an apology —myself and my friends.

[HILARY, *during following conversation, circles round and round* DAVIDS, *sometimes getting close to him and handling the revolver in his pocket, and then breaking away again impulsively.*]

DAVIDS. I reckon you do. Haven't you had any complaints from other people in the flats?

HILARY. No. They are accustomed to us. We are accustomed to them. This building is hardly the place that an exhausted city man would choose for a rest cure.

DAVIDS. Look here. I don't want any of your sarcasm. I've got it in my agreement that any tenant whose conduct is offensive to other residents in the building may be [*glancing at a pencilling on his cuff*] summarily ejected.

HILARY. And do you know that it is also in our respective agreements that coal may only be delivered on Saturday mornings, and then before ten o'clock; that dogs, live animals, actors, and hawkers are barred, and that broken whisky bottles may not be hurled from the windows at the heads of the passengers in the street? I do. Now, these restrictions, Mr. Davids, make life very complicated, don't they?

DAVIDS. Well, ain't it all necessary? What's the good of renting a place where you can't have a little peace and quiet when you want it?

HILARY. But do you want peace and quiet?

DAVIDS. Of course I do.

HILARY. How wonderfully interesting!

DAVIDS. When a man's been working hard all day he's earned his rest, and I'm damned well going to have it while I pay my rent here.

HILARY. I think you're deceiving yourself, Mr. Davids. You don't want peace and quiet. Oh, no you don't. The successful business man, in my experience, slumbers all day and wants to wake up at night. There is a ridiculous notion abroad that we are all tired when the day's work is done. It is quite false. The enervation of routine provokes a craving for excitement. Successful men, and all men are successful who work and are paid for working, are so blandly contented and cheerful during the daytime that they simply cannot resist the desire to do something strenuous at night. They must have excitement, as hectic as possible.

DAVIDS. I don't say that it isn't a relief to go to a musical comedy or some funny play during the evening after the storm and stress of business.

HILARY. But there is no storm and stress in business. Think it over. You and I know hosts of business men. We've worked with them and seen them working. Pallid, haggard lot, aren't they? Never seen 'em laugh, eh? Never seen 'em drink? Never hear 'em tell a risky story? Hair on end all day, isn't it? Nine o'clock to nine. No time for meals. No lengthy lunches with the typist. All rush, hustle, and worry, isn't it?

DAVIDS. Well, it ain't so bad as all that.

HILARY. No? That's a very frank admission from a business man. No, Mr. Davids, it is not in the least like that. Not more than one employer of labour in ten does more than a couple of hours' work a day. I don't reproach them. I abhor busy people. But I do think it is time that ridiculous old fairy tale were exposed. Look round at the entertainments at the theatres in London.

DAVIDS. Yes, nearly all light stuff. Something to make a man laugh and take him out of himself.

HILARY. Precisely. Doesn't it disgust you?

DAVIDS.   I don't see why it should.

HILARY.   Doesn't the success of these things
disgust you? The business man is told they're
good for him. Just the thing for his poor tired
brain. It flatters him. He doesn't in the least
know what a poor tired brain is, but it is so
splendidly British to believe you have one. People
simply adore being told that they are tired and
weary. They feel, oh! so interesting. And off
they go to the Gaiety to be cheered up. It's
true that they have been in a condition of semi-
hysterical cheerfulness all day, but that must never
be admitted. Now what people really want, Mr.
Davids, is to be harrowed. They would enjoy being
miserable, but they never dare admit anything of
the sort. Therefore the poor wretches are forced to
patronise musical comedy. On the stage what you
call the "light stuff" owes its success entirely to the
fact that John Bull will wear his hat over his eyes.

DAVIDS.   I didn't come up here to be told that. ֻI
came up to tell you what I thought of you, and
you've——

HILARY.   I've been analysing your complaint, and
have proved, I hope to your satisfaction, that you are
protesting under a misconception.

DAVIDS [stammering].   I don't know whether you
are trying to pull my leg or not.

HILARY.   Not for one moment, Mr. Davids. You
interest me.

DAVIDS [rather pleased].   Do I? I say, do you go
in for literary work—write for the papers and so on?

HILARY. No. I draw for the papers.

DAVIDS. Ha! An artist, eh? That's interesting. Where do you work? Not here?

HILARY. My studio is on the top floor.

DAVIDS. Got a studio, have you? I suppose you turn out a good bit.

HILARY. I keep pegging away.

DAVIDS. What sort of work do you do? Any painting, or only comic pictures?

HILARY. I paint a little. There is a picture of mine in this year's Academy.

DAVIDS. Go on!

HILARY. It's true. I don't want to deceive you.

DAVIDS. Then you're an R.A.

HILARY. Oh, no, no!

DAVIDS. But I thought that made you an R.A.

HILARY. Not necessarily. The stigma is avoidable.

DAVIDS. Well, there! Picture in the Academy, eh? No wonder you're a bit of a Bohemian. What do you paint? Girls?

HILARY. Very often.

DAVIDS. Then—I—er—I—er—suppose you employ models, eh?

HILARY. Frequently.

DAVIDS. Oh, you dog! [*chuckling and digging* HILARY *in the ribs*]. Ah, woman! lovely woman! Where would the world be without her?

HILARY. It is easy to imagine and terribly difficult to realise.

DAVIDS. There you go again. I'd have bet any-

thing you wrote for the papers. I shall have to drop
into your studio one day when it is convenient.

HILARY [*icily*].   That would be very pleasant.

DAVIDS.   You know I've artistic ideas myself, and
I do a bit of writing too.   I know I'm a draper, but
that isn't going to bar me from courting the Muses.
Would you like to see something I've written? [*pulling out a paper and giving it to* HILARY].

HILARY [*glancing at it*].   Poetry !

DAVIDS.   Yes.   You needn't read it all.   That's
the verse I like best [*indicating it*].

HILARY [*reading it*].

> " The scent of summer flowers she breathed,
>   Asleep on petals newly crushed—
>   A virgin wanton pose !
>   And gleams of tender bareness flushed
>   From amber veilings that enwreathed
>   Her skin of satin rose."

DAVIDS.   You do read it nicely.   What do you think
of it?

HILARY.   Disgusting ! [*handing back paper*].

DAVIDS [*doubtfully*].   Is it?   You don't think it
goes too far, do you?   I was going to send it to a
paper.

HILARY.   Don't.

> [HILARY *takes revolver from his pocket
> and puts it on desk R., putting
> newspaper over it.*

DAVIDS.   Have you ever written any poetry
yourself?

HILARY.   Once.   It took me a week to write and

polish it—four stanzas only. It was published and I was awarded a postal order for 7s. 6d.

DAVIDS. Ah, you mustn't look on the financial side of art. I am quite willing to pay for the publication of my poems. I'm sure most people have to. Have you got to-day's *Daily Mail*? Ah, is this it? [*rising and going to desk*]. Now, if any—Hello! [*noticing revolver*]. What's this? Is this your burglar scarer? Fully loaded too, ain't it?

HILARY. Yes. You interrupted my use of it when you came in.

DAVIDS. What? Have you had the burglars in?

HILARY. Oh, no. I was about to use it on myself.

DAVIDS. Ha, ha, ha! Going to commit suicide, eh? Ain't there a lot of it about just now?

HILARY [*smiling*]. I suppose there is. I'm in the fashion.

DAVIDS. It's a notion I could never understand. Mind you, I've had my morbid periods. But I cured myself in a very remarkable manner. Look here. [*He produces a booklet from his inside pocket.*] Have a look at this. [*Handing book to* HIL.] I compiled that myself.

HILARY [*examining book*]. *At the Sign of the Merrythought*, being a collection of optimistic epigrams and axioms, compiled from the works of famous authors by David Llewellyn Davids, J.P., L.C.C., M.A.B.

DAVIDS. And the arrangement is alphabetical.

HILARY. Quite so. [*Reading index*] "Art, Books, Cleverness, Death, Drink, Emotion, Fools, Friends,

Girls, Happiness, Heart, Honour, Ideals, Know-
ledge, Life, Love, Man, Marriage, Miscellaneous,
People, Personalities, Philosophy, Proverbs, Religion,
Sentiment, Theories, Thoughts, Troubles, Truth,
Vice, Virtue, Weather, Wisdom and Woman ! "

DAVIDS.   Threepence in paper, sixpence in cloth.
I paid for the publication, but I've had some of my
money back.   By compiling that book, I forced
myself to look always on the bright side of things.

HILARY.   I think it would depress me.

DAVIDS.   Not a bit.   You contemplate death.
Turn up page 42.   Quotations from the " Wreck of
the *Hesperus* " and "Casabianca."   Off you go to
lunch at Romano's.

HILARY [*laughing almost heartily*].   Hardly a
recipe for a poor man.

DAVIDS.   Suppose you've got indigestion.   Turn
up Miscellaneous !   Quotations from Brillat-Savarin
and Sir John Suckling.   Just the thing.   In five
minutes you're dancing the can-can and swooning
for food.   Nothing like dancing for the dumps.   I
once took a widow who had lost her fortune to a
Covent Garden ball.   She ate fourteen oyster patties
that night.   There was a waltz we had that I shall
never forget.   Let's see.   How did it go?   [*Hums
the air of a popular waltz.*]   Give me your hand.

> [*Takes* HILARY's *hand, puts his arm
> round his waist and waltzes awk-
> wardly with him, humming the
> tune the while.*
>
> [*Enter* PEEL *suddenly,* C.   *He places*

HILARY's *boots just inside the door,
blows his nose deprecatorily with a
large handkerchief and exit.*

DAVIDS [*bursting into a roar of laughter*]. That
old man tickles me no end. Well, don't you feel
better now, my boy? I'll tell you what we'll do.
We'll have a real Bohemian lunch. I'll run out and
get a good cold hamper and a couple of bottles of
bubbly—just to celebrate our acquaintance, eh?

HILARY. I can hardly refuse.

DAVIDS. Of course you can't, my boy We're
going to get on well together. You're just my
style. Don't care a damn for anybody, least of all for
yourself. Well, I shan't be more than a few minutes.

HILARY [*at window*]. I see it's raining heavily.
How does the *Sign of the Merrythought* help you
now?

DAVIDS. Here you are, my boy [*producing book*].
Page 72. "'There's a sun still shining in the sky.'
Pelissier."

[*Exit* DAVIDS, *C., almost colliding with*
JIM BENZIGER *who looks him over
superciliously.*

JIM [*closing door after* DAVIDS]. So the ogre has
paid his threatened visit.

HILARY. Yes. And, d'y'know, I rather like him.

JIM. Bought a picture?

HILARY. No, but probably would. I like his
way of laughing. It reminds you of big things. I
should like to take him into the heart of a Pyramid
and make him laugh at a mummified king.

JIM.   It looks as if he had cured you of that notion of suicide.

HILARY.   He has side-tracked it at any rate   I am going to have a good lunch at his expense, my boy, here—within these very walls.

> [*A sudden altercation is heard without between* PEEL *and* MAXIMILIAN CUTTS.

MAX.   I'm going in, I tell you.   I'm not a writ server, you old fool.   I'm Mr. Cutts' brother.

> [*Pulls C. door sharply open, bursts in, but stops sharp at the doorway.   He is a youngster of about twenty-three, and is rather dejected in appearance.   His shoulders are rounded and his carriage that of a bullied man.   He wears shabby serge, ill cut.   His brown boots are not brown.   He carries a bowler hat in his bare hands.   His face is very pale.   He has paper coverings on his cuffs.*

HILARY.   Max!

> [*Rises and extends his hand.*

MAX.   Hello, Hil.

> [*Taking it limply.*

HILARY.   What's brought you round ?

MAX.   I thought I'd——

> [*Looks deprecatingly round at* JIM, *who takes the hint.*

JIM. I'm off, Hilary. I shall look in later and sample the ogre's lunch.

HILARY. Right, Jim, and bring Will with you.

[*Exit C.*

HILARY. Sit down, Max. Fill your pipe.

MAX. No, thanks. I can't smoke.

[*Sits L.*

HILARY. Rats! Smoke, man, smoke.

MAX. Hil, old man, by God, I'm—I'm hungry.

HILARY [*reeling slightly and then standing motionless like a statue*]. Not breakfasted, eh? Careless devil. We'll soon see to that. [*Goes to tube and whistles.*] Is that you, Peel? Send me up another breakfast, bacon and eggs, toast and coffee. [*Goes down to* MAX *but not too near him.*] I'm damned sorry, Max.

MAX. All right, Hil. But it's been awful.

HILARY. I know, I know. But tell me how it happened. You had a job at a draper's, hadn't you? You told me that you got fifteen shillings a week and lived in.

MAX. I got the sack.

[*Enter* PEEL, *looking very miserable.*

PEEL. I beg your pardon, sir, but can I speak to you privately?

HILARY [*scenting what is coming*]. No, Peel. Shout it out.

PEEL [*brokenly*]. Well, sir, I beg your pardon, sir, but the mistress says you can't have any more breakfast until the last month's bills are paid.

HILARY. Thank you. Convey my compliments

D

to your mistress, and tell her that I have pleasure in cancelling the order.

> [*Exit* PEEL *on the verge of breaking into tears.*

MAX.   It's that way, Hil, is it?

HILARY.   Yes.

> [HILARY *goes to the sideboard and brings out a pot of jam, a bag of biscuits, and two apples.* MAX *spreads the jam on the biscuits with a spoon and eats ravenously.*

HILARY.   Why were you sacked, Max?

MAX.   They fired me for—for—a girl in the mantles. The first, Hil, the first. I'm twenty-three—and the first. We couldn't help it.

> ⸺ [*He chokes horribly over a dry biscuit.*

HILARY.   Heaven help you, dear old Max. Did you tell the management what you thought of them?

MAX.   What's the good? What's the good?

HILARY.   Max, you always miss your opportunities. I should rather have liked at the age of twenty-three to have been sacked for—for a girl in the mantles. It would have fired my eloquence. I should have said several things, quiet things, things that strike across the mouth and leave a trickle of blood. You are a pitiable figure, a poor man who doesn't know how to make the best of things.

MAX.   I would have done, Hil, but I haven't got your knack. I dry up when a man tells me I'm a dirty hound—and proves it.

HILARY.   Proves it.   Damn him!   Proves it.

Did he take his cigar out of his mouth while he said it ?   Did he fold his fat fingers, stare through you with his fishy eyes ?   I can see him serving out his sentence, Max.   Wasn't the room full of the wraiths of the poor anæmic little shop-girls that he had persecuted ?   Didn't you point them out to him ? Heaven bless my soul, why didn't you kill him ? You might have smashed him — smashed him ! These beasts never have any muscle.   You could have crushed his head, Max, under your thin, brown boots.   You could have mangled him.   Oh, how you've made me see blood !

MAX.   Don't get excited about it, Hil, old boy. It don't do any good.   And you mustn't forget our father kept big shops and made people live in.   He might have been like this brute.

HILARY.   He might.   He might.   He probably was, Max.   Our mother, you know, she——

MAX.   She forced him.

HILARY.   How the devil do you know ?

MAX.   We all know, don't we ?   She told Millicent one day, and Millicent has told us all at different times.

HILARY.   Ah !   What her life must have been like, eh, Max ?

MAX.   Awful.   Have you got any water ?

HILARY.   Yes, and better—a little whisky.

      [HILARY *gets him a long tumbler of*
                whisky and water.

HILARY.   What are you going to do now, Max ?

MAX.   Starve.

[*The man says it in an awful way.*
He means it.

HILARY.   Didn't he give you a character?

MAX.   Wasn't fool enough to ask for one after what he said.

HILARY.   What did he say?

MAX.   Said I was an unscrupulous scoundrel, that I couldn't afford to marry, and, therefore, had no right to have anything to do with women.   He reckoned I was one of the curses of civilisation, living just for amusement, he said I was.   Once I could have grinned at that.   But all the time he was speaking I was thinking "My living's gone— my living's gone."   He kept calling me a dirty hound.   I was blushing—burning.   It sounded as if he was right.   But he wasn't, was he, Hil?

[*For a moment* HILARY *does not answer.*
He sits very still in his chair.

HILARY.   I have never known the name of the shop you worked at.

MAX.   Davids, London Wall.

HILARY [*without any surprise*].   Davids, eh? David Llewellyn Davids?   Short?   Slightly corpulent?   Hair dressed like a barber's?   Fat hands? Big laugh?

MAX.   That's him.   Do you know him?

HILARY.   Life bristles with coincidences.   It's getting worse than the drama.   Yes, I know him.

MAX.   Oh, Hil, do you think you could get him to take me back?

HILARY [*almost shouting*].   Max!

MAX. Ah, Hil, I haven't got any principles left.
I couldn't bear to starve. It's not the pain of it, but
I want to live. I want just to live till——

HILARY. Till I die? [MAX's *head sinks between his
shoulders.*] Of course it is only natural.

MAX. I don't wish you harm, Hil. I swear I
don't. But I'm one of the youngest of our family,
mind. I'm at the age when money's wanted most,
and wanted for the things that young chaps want.
Most of you other boys have had your good time.
I've never tasted anything except school, and I hated
that because I wasn't strong. [*Helps himself to more
whisky and water.*] The other day I saw Dallas—
he went up from form to form with me. He was in
a car, a long car, with silver fittings, and he had a
girl with him, a little girl wrapped up in furs with
a pink face and gentle eyes. I watched them go by,
and, as I watched them, I could feel the hair on my
face that I couldn't afford to have shaved off. I felt
sick inside, and my head was light. By God, I shall
have a car some day.

> [MAX *is getting more and more
> excited under the influence of the
> whisky.*

HILARY. You suffer because you have no philosophy, no art to fall back on. I have had experi-
ences like that, but I am philosopher enough to find
satisfaction in such opulent displays. Envy is the
easiest pain in the world to assuage if you have
imagination.

MAX. I haven't got any art to help me. The

only thing I'm any good at is singing comic songs. I've had five bob more than once for singing at a pub smoker.

HILARY. Heavens, Max! Where did you learn to sing comic songs?

MAX. At the music hall. We could always go to the first house and get back in time.

HILARY. And you learnt those songs and sang them to beery audiences in public-houses. You, Maximilian Cutts, son of Sir Nathaniel Cutts?

MAX [chuckling mirthlessly]. Cutts, eh? That's funny. My name's Cutts, is it? I'd forgotten that.

HILARY. Forgotten it. What do you mean, Max?

MAX. I was known as Williams at the shop. You see the man who did my work before I came was called Williams. It saves a lot of confusion, and they always do it in draper's shops. The man who gets my job now will be called Williams, no matter what his name may be.

HILARY. What an extraordinary arrangement!

MAX. Is it? I've never thought about it. It made a difference to one of our chaps, though. He was the third from the door in the gloves, and the third from the door in the gloves is Mr. Sinclair, always has been and always will be. Well, he was secretly engaged to a girl in the ribbons, and not so long ago they moved him from the gloves to the vests and pants to take the place of a chap that died. Well, the dead chap was known as Mr. Green, so poor old Sinclair had to change his name to

Mr. Green.　And you'll hardly believe it, but the girl broke it off and took up with the new Sinclair.

> [*Helps himself to another glass of whisky.*

HILARY [*smiling*].　Then there's something in a name after all.

MAX.　Rather!　Cutts, indeed.　You could have called at that shop and asked for Cutts till you were black in the face.　Williams I was, second from the cash desk in the artificial flowers. . . . Still, I used to think of it at nights, Hil, when the other two fellows in my room didn't snore.　I used to lie awake and think of the money that's waiting —of just what I'd buy, and the sort of fine girl I'd marry.　And then the smell of that foul old barrack would get in my nose, and I'd curse you a bit, Hil. But only just as a brother would, old chap.

HILARY.　Don't excuse yourself, Max.　I know what it has meant for all of you.　I'm ashamed that I did not make up my mind before.

> [*The C. door is flung open and* DAVIDS *enters boisterously, singing* "*Bringing the Sunday dinner home.*"　*He carries a large hamper in his hands and under each arm is a bottle of champagne.　He comes down C. and places the hamper on the table C.*

DAVIDS.　Relieve me of the bubbly, or I'll drop it. [HILARY *goes to him and relieves him of the bottles.*] There's a game pie in here as big as a house.　You'll have to bring in some of your pals.   Hello! [*notic-ing* MAX] I didn't notice you had any company. Intro—Here!   I've seen this young fellow before.

HILARY.   This is my brother, Mr. Maximilian Cutts.

DAVIDS.   Remarkable likeness!   I took him for a young chap I had in my shop, called Williams.

MAX [*who has had sufficient whisky on an empty stomach to make him courageous*].   Yes, Williams— that's me—second from the cash desk in the artificial flowers.

DAVIDS.   What!   And you're this gentleman's brother?

HILARY.   Certainly, Mr. Davids.   You have no objection, I suppose, to his lunching with us.

DAVIDS.   Here—damn it!

MAX [*laughing mirthlessly*].   Lord bless you, Hil, what a notion!   Mr. David Llewellyn Davids lunch with his discharged employé!   Not a hope!

DAVIDS.   Here, I don't like this business.   Did you bring this brother of yours here on purpose?

HILARY.   He came to me because he was starving.

DAVIDS.   And serve him damned well right, too. The dirty little hound's not——

HILARY.   That's enough, Mr. Davids.   Your opinion on——

MAX.   Leave this to me, Hil [*going straight up to* DAVIDS *and speaking straight in his face*].   Look here, Mr. Davids, we're level now.   You can say what you like, but I can say what I like.   And I'm going to put you in your place.   How do you like that?

DAVIDS. The little beast's been drinking, hasn't he? [*to* HIL].

MAX. Drinking, eh? Well, it isn't your fault I'm not a corpse by now. You got rid of me, you kicked me out, but I'm going to get level.

DAVIDS [*turning disgustedly from* MAX *and going to* HIL]. I don't want anything to do with this fellow. If he's your brother, I'm sorry for you. You don't deserve it. But I like you, and I'll tell you why I got rid of him.

MAX. Oh, damn your explanations. I'm not going——

HILARY. Max, Max! There is plenty of time for that. Let us hear what Mr. Davids has to say.

DAVIDS [*dropping into a chair*]. Well, you've got to understand I'm not on my defence. But it'll do you good to hear my views. I've not been a master all my life. I know what I'm talking about. I've been in just a similar sort of position to this young fool. *I've* lived in a draper's shop and earned fifteen bob a week.

MAX. Yes, and look at you now. You're exactly what I've had to look forward to. With the best of luck I might one day become like you.

DAVIDS. What d'ye mean? I tell you I had fifteen bob a week and lived in, but I saved, and I've kept my hands clean. I saved and saved, and if a woman's face got in my way and made me feel weak, I punished myself by saving more. Sex-starvation, they call it. It's awful, but it can be done because it must be done. And everywhere it is done. The

Civil Service, for instance, is crowded with cases. There are one or two of them in every private firm. Some men it don't harm.   Others in middle age it drives to a phase of childish imbecility.   You've got to chance your luck and save your money till you can buy your partner.

HILARY.   And knowing all that, you are harsh on the boy of twenty-three who has not the character to wait—and wait—and risk his chance of imbecility.

DAVIDS.   Pardon me, sir, I know when a case should be treated harshly or not.   Look at that young rascal.   It's women, drink, cigarettes, and betting that make up his life.

MAX.   Liar! I never had anything to do with a girl before this one ; I swear it, Hil.

DAVIDS.   Of course you hadn't.   But you talked and dreamt of nothing else.   You sniggered over nothing else.   There was nothing else that drew you to music halls with your companions.   It was the one topic of conversation pretty nearly every time you sat down to a meal.   You'd even make coarse remarks about the lady customers you'd served. [*Turning to* HIL.]   What in Heaven's name is the good of that sort of breed ?   Is it any good to the country ?   You can tell me his sin was natural. But so is all sin.   It's the unnatural people and our unnatural laws that make existence possible.   A pretty state of affairs we should come to if employers were to overlook vice of that description—because it couldn't be helped.   It can be helped.

HILARY.   Yes, Mr. Davids.   If you catch a mouse,

you kill it. But can you blame the mouse for being caught?

DAVIDS. How d'ye mean? I don't bait traps.

HILARY. No, but you keep the mice too close to the cat.

DAVIDS. Pah! Men and women have to mix. I've no respect for these blessed Turks with the harems and veiled women. A lot of cowards, that's what they are.

HILARY. I don't suggest that you should segregate the sexes entirely. But it's not good that men and women should be together all day when they are young. It is not good that they should be employed on similar work. If Mabel sells ribbons on one side of the shop, George should not be selling artificial flowers on the other side.

DAVIDS. Why?

HILARY. Mabel thinks she is as good as George, and George thinks he is no worse than Mabel. The sexes were never meant to be equal. Either man or woman must be accepted as the superior. If woman *en masse* insisted on absolute equality with man there would be considerable fecundity—but a slump in population. If she insisted on superiority, all would be well. But there is no hope of that. Women are so selfish.

MAX [*who has been sitting with his face buried in his arms during this argument, now lifts his head impulsively. There are tears in his eyes, maudlin tears of self-pity*]. Oh, God, how you talk. I've slid into the mud and you talk and talk to this

devil. Talk, talk, talk, and I'm starving. And
that fat hog sits between us with his hamper and
his champagne posing as a censor of morals. Why
don't you kick him out?

DAVIDS. See here, young man. What do you
think is going to happen to that young woman you
ruined?

HILARY. Steady, Mr. Davids, perhaps she ruined
herself.

DAVIDS. I don't care. He's legally responsible.
That young woman's got to go away. She ain't a
bad young woman, and I'll have her back. But
who's going to pay? I am. She hasn't got any
parents, so I've got to. D'ye think I don't run
risks doing that? Doesn't it get talked about?
Not for me to hear, mind you. It does get
talked about and I get the blame. Has that side
struck you, you little fool?

HILARY. You ought to pay. You're to blame in
the beginning. You didn't start this system, but
you perpetuate it in its worst form, so you must
take its kicks with its halfpence.

DAVIDS. Oh, I'm to blame, am I? Well, suppose
I don't pay. Suppose I turn the girl out and put
the police on this young blackguard.

HILARY. You daren't. It's to your interest to
hush up all your shop scandals. You know that
public opinion would insist on a clean sweep of all
such places if the real facts were known. In fact,
you're only too anxious to pay.

MAX. Yes, by God, and I could tell a story if

they put me to it.   What happened to Miss Edwards and Miss Norrys and Miss——

DAVIDS.   Shut your mouth, you young fool.   You don't know what you're talking about.

MAX.   I do know, Mr. Davids.   And I'm going to let other people know.   I'm not going to be a pauper always.   Don't you worry about that.   My day is coming, and my first job will be to expose you.

DAVIDS [*laughing loud and harshly*].   See here, you petty whimperer, I've had many such a threat before—yes, from quite grown-up people.   My life's not been spotlessly clean, but any man can run it over with a rule.   Women have suffered for me, but, by George, I don't owe any of 'em a halfpenny.   As you grow older you'll find out that you can wrong your fellow-creatures and be positively applauded if you open your purse wide enough afterwards.   But you've got to have the money in your pocket before you sin.   Paupers mustn't break the laws either of God or man [*to* HILARY].   I'm not concerned with the justice or injustice of the theory, but with the facts.

HILARY.   Ah, yes, the old story.   Take life as you find it, not as you know you ought to lead it. I don't dislike you, Davids, but you are conspicuously a curse to your fellow-creatures.

DAVIDS.   Yes, you're a pretty fine theorist, aren't you?   Champagne and chicken [*pointing to the table*] are a curse, aren't they?   If I bought a picture from you, that would be a curse, wouldn't it?   I reckon this young man is a little more material.

MAX. Damn your food !

DAVIDS [*mockingly*]. "Give us this day our daily bread."

MAX [*grabbing champagne bottle by the neck, but not lifting it*]. Get out of this or I'll kill you.

HILARY. Max, drop that.

               [MAX *lets go of the bottle.*

DAVIDS. Ah, anything but that. Let him drink to his own destruction when I'm gone. [*Picking up his hat.*] Look here, young man. [*Addressing* MAX *and pressing on him till he retreats to the writing-desk. Here* MAX *stands with his back to the desk and his hands resting on it—the right hand in close proximity to the revolver.*] I've got rid of you, and I don't want to see you again. I warn you that if you are a nuisance to me I'll break you. I've had the handling of little hounds of your sort before, and I know how to set about 'em. [*Turns from* MAX *to* HIL *and stands between table and settee.*] I'm sorry our acquaintance has come to such an abrupt ending, but you're a bad hand at choosing relations.

        [MAX *fires from desk into* DAVIDS' *back.*
           HILARY *is sitting on chair on left*
              of table C.

DAVIDS [*his jaw dropping*]. My God ! You've hit me.

           [DAVIDS *drops to the floor where he*
            stands and remains hunched up by
            the table. Both MAX *and* HILARY
            hurry to him and lift him. They
            drop him as if frightened.

HILARY.   He's dead!

MAX.   Dead!   Listen to his heart.   [HILARY *bends over the body.*]   There is some one coming.   They've heard the shot.   Hil!   Hil!   I shall be hanged.

HILARY.   You!   You! . . . Max, give me the revolver.   [MAX *hands it over.*]   Help me!   Help me to lie.

> [*Half collapses into chair behind table C.*   PEEL *bursts into the room.* MAX *shrinks down settee to extreme end.*

PEEL.   Mister Cutts!   Mister Cutts!   Oh!   [*seeing body*].

> [JIM *and* WILL *hurry in anxiously.*

JIM.   Good God!   Hilary!   What's happened?

HILARY.   I shot him, Jim.   I've killed him.   It was a way out!

CURTAIN

ACT III

[The scene is the same as in Acts I. and II. The disposition of the furniture is the same, but there are changes apparent in the room such as would naturally be expected to occur in the course of some months. It is now summer. A gaily coloured screen is in front of the fireplace where a fire had been burning brightly in the first two Acts. There are a few flowers in a vase on the mantel-shelf. A great number of newspapers are piled about the room. Carelessly pinned up over the sideboard, R. of door C., is an evening newspaper's contents bill, reading "TRIAL OF HILARY CUTTS: VERDICT." When the curtain rises JIM BENZIGER *is seen seated in easy-chair by fireplace, down L., reading a newspaper.* WILL GRAIN *is at desk R., writing.* PEEL *stands by chair above table C., and is reading aloud from a newspaper. As usual, when he reads, his black-rimmed spectacles are pushed up on his forehead and the paper is held close to his eyes.]*

PEEL *[reading]*. "Something concerning the personality of Herbert Burridge, the man entrusted with tó-morrow's execution, cannot fail to be of interest to our readers. [JIM *and* WILL *make gestures of impatience*.] He is by profession a hairdresser and umbrella repairer, and, when not in the receipt of His Majesty's commands, resides at Chorley. Workmen and their wives and children are to be seen entering and leaving his establishment day after day, and their countenances betray no feelings of dread at their so doing. They don't approach the shop with fear and tremor, neither do they leave it as though released from a dungeon."

WILL. Ah, burn the thing, Peel.

JIM. No, no. Go on, Peel. That sort of journalism is really indirectly criminal. Criminology entrances me.

PEEL. "Burridge is a most humane man of retiring disposition, and as customers lie at his mercy when he has a razor in hand, they do so unflinchingly." It's nice to think that poor Mr. Cutts will be handled sympathetically at the end, isn't it?

JIM. Most consoling, Peel. Any more of it?

PEEL [*scrutinizing paper*]. One and a half columns, including the portrait.

JIM. Good gracious. [*Takes paper from* PEEL.] Listen to this, Will. "Burridge goes to perform an execution the same as if he were going to feed his chickens or cut a person's hair. He is always perfectly calm, and his razor, when shaving, does not betray any signs of nervousness. His appetite is always the same. He eats well, but he never changes his diet before going to or after returning

E

from an execution. He does not eat large beef-steaks, potatoes with thick gravy, nor strong drinks. He takes no drink at all, and the food he eats is always simple and wholesome. In short, although a hangman, he is no different from other men."

PEEL. Well, there now. I wonder, by the way, how one becomes a hangman.

WILL. The man who wrote that rot ought to be hanged himself.

JIM. The man who wrote that rot ought to be delivered into my hands. I should like to lodge and board him for some time, so that I could leisurely analyse him. He is a pervert, of course.

WILL. Probably a woman.

JIM. No. Sexless, I should imagine. It should be made to talk and write constantly. It should be allowed to develop its ego. There is a certain type of journalist whose depths of depravity have never been sounded. For the sake of discovering his possibilities, a specimen should be trapped and diplomatically nursed. It should not take long to discover the limitations of his viciousness.

WILL. What good would that do?

JIM. Good? Good? I don't want to do good. Why will you insist on mistaking all your intelligent friends for members of the Fabian Society?

WILL [*sticking down an envelope and handing letter to* PEEL]. Post that for me at once, will you, PEEL?

PEEL [*who has been standing with his hand on the handle of the door C., but listening most interestedly to the conversation.*] Certainly, sir.   [*Exit* PEEL, *C.*

WILL.   Ah've written a last line to Hilary.

JIM.   What, precisely, did you say?

WILL [*shamefacedly*].   Ah told him the latest news and Ah told him—well—just all that a chum could say to a chum that's got to swing.   The real truth of that crime has got to be told to the world when he's dead.   Ah'm not going to have him remembered as a common felon.

JIM.   The real truth?   Are you sure you know the real truth?

> [*Enter* MAXIMILIAN CUTTS, *C. He presents
> a considerably improved appear-
> ance. He carries his head better,
> his cheeks are fatter, and his voice
> has a confident ring. He wears
> the same suit, but carries a stick
> and is smoking a cigarette. On
> his head is a new straw hat with
> a black band. He enters briskly,
> throws down hat and stick, and
> seats himself in chair above table C.*

MAX.   Good evening, Mr. Benziger.   Good evening, Mr. Grain.   Had dinner?

JIM.   No.

WILL.   No.

MAX.   Are you going to grub out?

JIM.   Hardly.

WILL [*going up to him*].   Do you feel like " grubbing out " as you call it?

MAX.   I feel hungry.   I suppose I oughtn't to, but I do.

WILL. You can feel as hungry as you like, and eat what you like, and do what you like, but let me tell you that your beastly flippancy is not particularly pleasant to your brother's friends this evening.

MAX. I don't admit being flippant. I'm rational. That's all.

WILL [*blazing with rage*].   Rational !   Do you call your conduct since your brother's conviction rational ? You're the most unnatural, self-centred little beast Ah've ever come across. For two pins Ah'd thrash the life out of you.

MAX. And my answer is that you are a silly, sickly sentimentalist. You belong to the order of fools who wear black clothes as a token of mourning and pile immortelles on the coffin of a statesman who dies of drink.

JIM. Why shouldn't he die of drink ?

MAX. No reason whatever. Quite a philosophic death, but regarded by your inconsistent immortelle-scatterer as entirely loathsome. [*Turning to* GRAIN.] You seem to look upon me as an unnatural beast because I do not openly grieve over my brother's approaching execution. Let me tell you, I welcome my brother's death, though I deplore the manner of it. But am I responsible for the manner of it ?

WILL. You've got me there. Ah put the idea into his head.

MAX. So you did, but you were afraid to say so in the witness-box.

WILL. It would have ruined me. And it wasn't necessary.

MAX. Quite so. It was unnecessary. Hilary confessed all, told his own story, and I—and I alone—had to swear that he fired the shot with intent to kill.

JIM. How in God's name you did it, I don't know. I've seen some remarkably nonchalant murderers under trial, but I never expected to see a man swear away his brother's life with such—after-dinner geniality.

MAX. How would you have had me behave? Was I to shiver, look 'pale, droop my eyelids to satisfy a fatuous public notion of decency? Decency! Pah!

JIM [*thoughtfully*]. Decency—decency. A good name for a play.

MAX. I behaved as I felt. And I felt glad. Hilary was to die, and he deliberately chose to die that way. I and my unfortunate brothers and sisters were on the edge of happiness. Only a hypocrite would have affected concern. Besides, there was plenty of comedy for me in that final scene. When the judge said to Hilary, "May the Lord have mercy on your soul," the memory came back to me of old Hil in a comic costume riding a donkey at our village sports. Just as the chaplain said "Amen," I recalled how the donkey bucked and threw old Hil off. He must have been thinking of something equally funny, because his eye caught mine and he laughed outright. I shall never forget his Lordship's shocked face.

JIM.   That was certainly amusing.   His Lordship has such a reputation as a humorist, too.   But still, he was not present at the village sports, I take it.

MAX.   Yes, he was, in the abstract.   So were you, and so was Grain.   You all roared when Hil fell off the donkey, and you all mope at the idea of the six-foot drop.   Can't death be comic?

WILL.   Look here, young man, Ah'm sick of you and your blasphemous talk.   Your brother was my friend and Ah—damn you!

[*Snatches up his hat and exit* C.

MAX.   H'm, I'm sorry I offended him.   My views are eccentric, I suppose.   He's not accustomed to that sort of thing in the House of Commons.   One must have phlegm nowadays.   You've got it.

JIM.   I'm a little in advance of my time, perhaps. I don't ruffle when I'm bored.   I simply feel faint.

MAX.   I don't bore you.   I know I don't.   I can feel you studying me.   I have always felt it.

JIM.   What makes you think that death can be comic?

MAX.   I never thought it until this particular instance arose.   But I must confess that it has amused me in fiction.   I laughed at the conclusion of *A Tale of Two Cities.*   Sydney Carton on the scaffold is to my mind an irresistibly comic figure. I admire his heroism, mind you, but as one of the spectators in the know, I chuckle over the absurdity of his execution.

JIM.   Why does your brother's fate remind you of Sydney Carton?

MAX [*a little confused*].   Oh—well—Hilary, after all, is sacrificing himself for others.   He did not want to kill this man Davids.

JIM.   And because he killed Davids for impersonal motives, and got himself condemned to death for it, you regard to-morrow's execution as comic.

MAX.   Certainly ; because the law and the world are being fooled.   You must see the humorous side of it.   Don't tell me you agree with Mr. Grain.   I am bitterly sorry that Hilary is to die because he's my brother.   But I am heartily glad that by means of his execution my other brothers and sisters whom I love equally well are to be rescued from the direst misery.

JIM [*slowly*].   I don't see your point.   I entirely fail to see the comedy of this death.   When I saw Hilary in prison, I asked him how he regarded the prospect.   I never lose an opportunity, I may mention, of improving my psychological knowledge. Hilary said—and mind you his sense of humour is as keen as yours—that, reviewing life as he had ex-perienced it, its end was its most wholesome feature. Wholesome, that was the word he used.   Life is comic, I grant.   But death is only wholesome.

MAX [*rising*].   Well, you won't be convinced, I can see, so it's no use talking about it.   By the way, there is something I had forgotten to mention.   I hope you won't think I have taken a liberty.   A fr—— an acquaintance of mine is calling this even-ing—on business.   I know I ought to have asked your permission.   But you have been good enough

to let me live here since the police allowed you to
return to the flat, and I thought I might ask him to
come in.

JIM.   Who is he?

MAX.   He's a money-lender.

JIM.   Hilary told me that you could not anticipate.

MAX.   This man is letting me have a small sum at
his own risk.

JIM.   Can't you wait for your money?

MAX.   I'm afraid I can't.   We shan't be able to
touch the governor's money for some time, and this
fellow is obliging me.

JIM.   How much are you borrowing?

MAX.   Fifty pounds.

JIM.   What sort of interest is he charging?

MAX.   It's rather heavy, but I want the money
to-night.   He said if I waited till to-morrow, till
after Hilary was dead, he would let me have it for
a mere 15 per cent or so.

JIM.   Why must you have the money to-night?

MAX.   You know that girl—the girl I got sacked
for?

JIM.   Yes.

MAX.   Davids was going to look after her, but
when he was killed she had to get another job.
She's found me out, and she swears she'll go to a
solicitor if I don't pay her something substantial
to-night.   I must do it.   It would spoil all my life
if that beastly business were to come out just as I
came into the money.

JIM.   Why must *she* have it to-night?

MAX. She's got a job as a cashier. She's been robbing the till. If she doesn't put it back to-night, she'll be caught. Oh, I do hope you won't mind. I have been so worried about it.

JIM. Why must he come here? Why not deal with him at his office?

MAX. I suppose I must tell you. He's a queer, morbid sort of chap. It seems he's very keen on murder trials, and all sorts of criminal cases. He told me he was in court all through Hilary's trial. He recognised my name and the address, and pressed me to let him see the room where the murder took place. I tried to put him off, but at last he made it a condition to his lending the money before Hilary's death. I had to give in. You'll let him come in, won't you?

JIM. For that wretched girl's sake, I will.

MAX. Thanks so much. You're awfully good to me.

JIM. Not at all. Sit down [*indicating settee on R.*]. Let us resume that very interesting discussion. What makes you think that death can be comic?

MAX. Well, really, aren't you tired of the subject? The thing's plain enough to me.

JIM. That is why I want you to expound. I suppose I'm very dense this evening. But the suggestion tickles me. Let me explain my difficulty by means of a parallel example. If, when I was a boy at school, I indulged in some lawless escapade and got off scot-free, certainly I was amused. And if another boy, perfectly innocent, were punished for my misdemeanour, I agree that I laughed immoderately.

MAX.   Well, there you are !

JIM [*very piercingly*].   How do you mean — " There you are " ?

MAX [*nervously*].   Aren't the cases similar ?   You said yourself that it was a parallel example.

JIM.   *I* said so.   Do *you* say so ?

MAX.   Well, in one way, of course.

JIM.   Think now.   Why did I laugh ?   I laughed because another boy was being punished for my sin. Do you laugh because Hilary is being punished for some one else's sin ?

MAX.   I don't laugh at all.   I say there is comedy in Hilary's fate because it is the direct result of a crime which he never wanted to commit.

JIM.   I don't understand.   Your evidence at the trial was to the effect that he did want to kill Davids and did it in cold blood.

MAX.   Yes, I know, but——

JIM.   But what ?

MAX.   He would have killed anybody to get——

JIM.   To get himself killed ?   I don't believe it. Neither did the jury, I'll swear.   Hilary was sentenced to death because your evidence made it plain that he killed Davids to avenge your ill-treatment.

MAX [*by now very frightened*].   Well ?

JIM.   Well, is that comic ?   Is it comic that your brother should hang because he championed you in your misery ? . . . You don't answer.   It is not comic.   No human being could see comedy in that sort of situation. Therefore, it is not the true state of affairs. You must have perjured yourself in the witness-box, or there would be nothing for you to laugh at.

MAX. I told the truth. You know that Mr. Grain put the idea into his head of getting hanged for murdering some public scourge.

JIM. Yes, yes. I know the story. I know what Grain said. But Hilary's subsequent action proves that he did not take his advice. Having murdered Davids, why didn't he blow his own brains out, instead of going through the horrors of a trial and execution?

MAX. I daresay he would have done if he'd thought of it.

JIM. I don't think he had time to think of it. Davids did not attack him, I suppose?

MAX. No.

JIM. Did Davids attack you?

MAX. No.

JIM. Then, Hilary, if he shot Davids at all——

MAX. Of course he shot him.

JIM. Well, you know, of course. You are the only one who does know the facts. You are, to use your own phrase in connection with Sydney Carton's execution, "one of the spectators in the know." Was there a third witness present when Davids was shot?

MAX [*intensely scared at the suggestion*]. Good Heavens, no!

JIM. Then *you* shot him, you little rat. That's

what you find so comic. When the judge prayed God to have mercy on Hilary's innocent soul, your sense of humour was tickled, little rat. I'm not surprised [*grabbing him by the coat - collar and shaking him*], little rat.

MAX. Let me go. You're mad. I didn't kill him. I swear I didn't kill him.

JIM. Listen, little rat. It's your word against his. If Hilary accuses you, you're under as great a suspicion as he.

MAX. Hilary never said that. He didn't. [*Getting hysterical.*] He didn't. He promised he——

JIM [*sharply*]. Promised he—what?

MAX [*realising that he has committed himself*]. Oh, you devil! [*bursts into hysterical tears*].

JIM. You flatter me.

MAX. You're not going to tell this story. You're not going to—you shan't! Hilary has confessed. He'll hang to-morrow. You can't hang two men for one crime. Can you? Can you? You can't. I swear you can't. For God's sake, don't start the story. It'll ruin me. It won't do any good. You don't want me hanged, do you? I never did it. I swear I never did it. Hilary shot him. But it might look bad for me if you were to tell. You won't tell, will you? Oh, say you won't tell. Look here. You're not rich. I shall be. You can have——

> [JIM *knocks him down with a blow across the mouth.*

JIM. Get up, little rat. Now listen to me for a

few moments. I suspected that you were the real
murderer when I burst into the room a few moments
after Davids was shot. I suspected from your manner
then and your manner since. Hilary's manner convinced me that the truth was not told at the trial.
When I interviewed him in prison, I put my sus-
picions as plainly as possible in the presence of the
warders. Hilary did not deny, nor did he affirm,
but he begged me to let things go. "I've got to
die," he said, "and you'll be a bad friend if you do
anything to prevent it." So you're safe, little rat.
I've given my word that I will not hinder your
brother's execution. Oh, you're safe enough.

MAX [*after a pause*]. I suppose I've got to clear
out of here.

JIM. Certainly not. I want you a little longer.
You were quite right when you said I was studying
you. I am. And I want to keep you under the
microscope for a few hours more at any rate.

[*Enter* WILL GRAIN, C. MAX *slinks into
his bedroom, formerly* HILARY'S,
off L.]

JIM. What's brought you back, Will?

WILL. Jim, Ah couldn't sit by myself. Ah couldn't
bear to be alone and just keep thinking and thinking
of poor old Hil in his cell. It chokes me. Ah feel
as bad as he must feel.

JIM. I don't think you understand Hilary, much
as you love him. Hilary, I am sure, is not now
grieving over his approaching demise. He is just
wondering whether his death will do his relations

any good.   I have never come across a man so
genuine in his contempt for mere existence.

WILL.   You're wrong, Jim.   A man can't sit over-
night and wait for the hangman without sweating
with fear.   It's such a loathsome death.   There
never has been a murder so cruel as the sentence of
a British judge.

JIM.   I suppose you would abolish capital punish-
ment.

WILL.   No, far from it.   But Ah'd only sentence a
murderer to be hanged after a delay of a fortnight,
if it were proved that the murderer had treated his
victim in the same way.   If a man locked up his
wife, told her that at the end of a fortnight he'd
cut her throat, and carried out his threat at the
appointed time, then he'd deserve to be hanged
after the manner of the British judicial system, but
only then.   Murderers rarely torture their victims.
They simply kill them.   Our laws both torture and
kill.

> [*Enter* PEEL, *C.   He carefully closes the
> door behind him and comes down
> C., then speaking in a very con-
> fidential manner.*

PEEL.   A person has called to see Mr. Maximilian
Cutts.   Should he be admitted, sir?

JIM.   What's his name?

PEEL [*consulting visiting-card*].   Mr. Stuart Campbell.

JIM.   A Scotsman?

PEEL.   Perhaps, sir.   He looks to me, sir, like

one of those gentlemen that Mr. Hilary always wanted to examine through the keyhole first.

JIM. I think I know who he is. A money-lender, Will. The young fool made an appointment with him here to-night.

WILL. Durned impudence.

JIM. I gave him permission. Show him in, Peel.

PEEL [*resignedly*]. If you approve, sir.

[*Exit* PEEL, *C.*

WILL. I suppose they want the room to themselves.

JIM. Let 'em want. I shan't allow it.

[*Enter* PEEL, *C.*

PEEL [*announcing*]. Mr. Stuart Campbell.

[*Enter* MR. STUART CAMPBELL, *C. He is a slim man of medium height and pronouncedly Hebraic features. He wears a grey bowler hat and carries a small bag.*

CAMPBELL. Good evening, gentlemen.

JIM [*who is sitting in chair by fire, reading*]. Good evening.

WILL [*who is seated on settee*]. Good evening.

CAMPBELL. Is Mr. C. in?

[*Exit* PEEL, *C.*

JIM. Mr. —— who?

CAMPBELL. Mr. C. Mr. M. C. Mr. Maximilian Cutts. We always call gents by their initials in my profession. There's a feeling that when you're doing a little friendly business it's more respectful. I don't know how it strikes you.

[MR. CAMPBELL *speaks softly and
            sibilantly.*

        [JIM *rises and goes to bedroom door, L.*

JIM. Cutts, your acquaintance has arrived.

                        [*Returns to seat.*

        [MAX *enters nervously from L.*

MAX [*looking out of the corner of his eye at* JIM *and*
WILL]. Good evening, Mr. Campbell. These are
my friends, Mr. Benziger and Mr. Grain. [CAMPBELL
bows to these gentlemen's backs.] I see you are well up
to time.

CAMPBELL. Yes, Mr. C. I always keep my watch
five minutes fast in case I should disappoint a
customer. Gents who require temporary financial
assistance like prompt dealing. They get it from
some firms, not from all. But you know the right
turning off Piccadilly, don't you, Mr. C.? Well,
let's get to business. Is this the room where the
murder was committed?

        [WILL *snorts indignantly, but* JIM *only
            pricks up his ears and listens
            interestedly.*

MAX [*wretchedly*]. Yes, Mr. Campbell, it was here.
Have you brought the—er—agreement?

CAMPBELL. Both the agreement and the money,
Mr. C. Can you see the bloodstains?

MAX. Do take a seat, Mr. Campbell.

CAMPBELL. Certainly, Mr. C. [*Sitting on chair
above table, C.*] Perhaps you are right. Business
first and pleasure afterwards. Well, well. There's
the agreement, Mr. C. [*producing paper from bag*].

Read it over, and satisfy yourself that it's quite
O.K., Mr. C.

> [MAX *takes paper and looks through it,
> while* MR. CAMPBELL *surveys the
> room with beady eyes.*

CAMPBELL. It don't look murderish, this room.
At the trial I never got the opinion it was a room
like this. But there you are. Realism is always
disappointing. Yes, Mr. C. [*answering a muttered
query from* MAX]. That's the ordinary rate of interest
in these cases.

MAX. How much are the expenses?

CAMPBELL. The enquiry fee, Mr. C., in your case,
will be one guinea and a half, sixpence for the agreement, ten shillings and ninepence for my travelling
expenses, and two pounds ten shillings the precautionary insurance. [MAX *gapes at him, but* CAMPBELL's
eyes wander round the room again.] Was there a
struggle?

MAX. What on earth is the precautionary insurance?

CAMPBELL. Well, Mr. C., for two pounds ten
I can insure your life for fifty pounds for a year,
and that would save any unpleasantness with your
executors in case of your death. It's always done.
My clients prefer it.

MAX. But the agreement is for seventy pounds.
I only wanted fifty pounds for a year.

CAMPBELL. That amount, Mr. C., includes the
interest.

MAX. Forty per cent!

F

CAMPBELL.   I assure you, Mr. C., it's necessary. We often lose everything we lend.

MAX.   Then if I sign this, I agree to pay you seventy pounds at the end of a year?

CAMPBELL.   That is so, Mr. C.

MAX.   And how much do I get?

CAMPBELL.   Fifty pounds, less expenses, Mr. C.; to be exact, forty-five pounds seven shillings and three-pence.

MAX.   But it's preposterous.

CAMPBELL.   I hope you haven't wasted my time, Mr. C.

MAX.   Give it to me.   I'll sign it.

> [*He takes the agreement, crosses to writing-desk and signs it, returning it to* MR. CAMPBELL.

CAMPBELL.   Thank you, Mr. C.   [*Producing bank-notes and gold.*]   Have you got change of half-a-sovereign?

MAX.   No.   Haven't you?

CAMPBELL.   I'm afraid not, Mr. C.

MAX [*after glancing hesitatingly at* JIM *and* WILL]. I'll run across to the Post Office and get it.

> [*Picks up his hat and exit* C.
> [*Some seconds' pause.* CAMPBELL *peers about the room, stares at the backs of* JIM *and* WILL, *and then, suddenly, in heavily punctuated syllables, asks a question.*

CAMPBELL.   Where did the body drop?

> [WILL *jumps up as if to expostulate*

with CAMPBELL, *but a sign from*
JIM *restrains him. A heavy silence
again follows.*

CAMPBELL. Do either of you gents know the
time of the execution?

JIM. Mr. Cutts will tell you all you wish to
know when he returns.

[*Again a silence. The telephone bell
rings.* JIM *rises leisurely and
goes to it.*

JIM. Yes? This is Mr. Benziger. No. Mr.
Cutts is out. He will be back in a moment if you care
to hang on. Who are you? Darragh and Davis?
`Oh, yes, I know. Mr. Hilary Cutts' solicitors.
What? Good what? Good news? Home
Secretary interfered. Mr. Cutts' sentence commuted.
Good God, Will. [*Turning to* GRAIN.] Hilary's
not to hang. It's penal servitude for life. [*Back
to telephone.*] What? Are you sure? You've just
had the message. Right, right, right! I'll tell
him.

[*Puts down telephone receiver.*

WILL. Jim, Jim, Ah hoped for it, but Ah never
dared say so. Thank God! Thank God! And he
won't be in long if Ah can do anything in Parliament.
Ah'll have him out before he knows he's in. Ah'll——

[*Enter* MAX, C. *He puts down his hat,
looks curiously at* WILL, *and comes
down to the table.* JIM *is again
down L., and is sitting in his chair
with his head in his hands.* WILL,

glowing with relief, is standing R.
of table.   When MAX *enters* WILL
drops down R. below settee.

MAX.   Here is the money.   [CAMPBELL, *who has*
been sitting half stupefied by the news, looks up re-
proachfully at MAX *and gathers up his notes and gold.*]
What are you doing that for?

CAMPBELL.   H'm, Mr. C., I think it's safer in my
pocket.

MAX [*slightly alarmed*].   What?   Aren't you going
to lend me the money?   Have they been trying to
put you off?

[*Turning angrily to* WILL *and* JIM.

CAMPBELL.   Oh, no, Mr. C.   But information has
come to hand showing the security to be bad.   Con-
sequently we can't do business.

MAX.   What do you mean?   I must have it, I
tell you.   You promised——

CAMPBELL.   Mr. C., your friends have some news
for you.

MAX.   News!   What news?

JIM [*looking up*].   A message has just come
through on the telephone from Hilary's solicitors.

MAX.   Yes?

JIM.   The Home Secretary has commuted Hilary's
sentence into penal servitude for life.

MAX [*muttering at first*].   Commuted!   Penal
servitude!   Not hanged!   It's a lie!   You devils,
it's a lie!

WILL.   It's the truth, and thank God for it!

MAX.   The truth!   Hilary's not to die!   Hilary's

not to die! [*He laughs mirthlessly.*] It's absurd. He was sentenced. The jury found him guilty. Twelve men found him guilty in twelve minutes. Twelve in twelve. No recommendation to mercy. " To be hanged by the neck till you are dead." The judge said so. Yes, he'll be dead to-morrow. [*Suddenly shouting.*] What do you mean by lying to me?

JIM [*raising his head*]. Listen!

> [*Through the open window is heard the shout of a newsboy.*

" Hilary Cutts Reprieved — Home Secretary's Decision—Hilary Cutts Reprieved."

> [MAX *stands with dropped jaw and stupefied limbs.*

CAMPBELL [*rising from table, shutting his bag and picking up his hat*]. I'm sure this will be a great relief for you, Mr. C., although I have to disappoint you about the money. In the circumstances, if it's only to show my sympathy, that is to say, my gratification, I'll waive the little matter of expenses. Good day, Mr. C. Good day, Mr. B. Good day, Mr. G. [*Exit* CAMPBELL, C.

MAX [*who has watched* CAMPBELL's *departure as if the figure of the man fascinated him*]. I don't get the money! [*Suddenly shouting again.*] Why is he reprieved?

JIM. Buy the evening paper.

MAX. It's a conspiracy. It's a damnable conspiracy. There's something at the bottom of this. Somebody wants to stop us getting that money.

Hilary's been trapped. We've got to go on—to go on going down. We can all go to the devil again. Oh, my God !

> [PEEL *suddenly bursts into the room waving an evening newspaper triumphantly.*

PEEL [*breathlessly*]. Mr. Benziger ! Mr. Grain ! He's reprieved. He's——

> [*Stops short at the sight of* MAX.

MAX [*standing just above table C., an awful picture of despair*]. What am I going to do ? What am I going to do ? What are we all going to do ?

> [JIM *makes a noise in his throat something like a laugh.*

CURTAIN

Printed by R. & R. CLARK, LIMITED, *Edinburgh.*

LOVE—AND WHAT THEN?

shows the revolt of the youthful and light-hearted wife of an austere provincial clergyman, whom she shocks by her insistence on appearing at an entertainment of his parishioners in a very short-skirted costume. Further, she flirts rather dangerously with a young naval lieutenant, but is saved from irreparable error by the intervention of a kindly and unconventional Bishop.

"One of the smartest modern comedies we have read for many a day. The dialogue from first to last shines with sparkling wit, and the plot shows outstanding originality of construction."—*Dundee Advertiser*.

Cloth, 2s. net; Paper, 1s. net.

THE TIDE

"an emancipated melodrama," as the author calls it, tells of the romantic career of Felicity Scarth, who at eighteen was robbed of her illegitimate child, at twenty-one became rich and attempted to stifle her craving for the child by a life of dissipation, and at thirty-four attempted suicide to end everything. By the help of a doctor she rediscovers her child, now a grown girl of eighteen, and after further trials all ends happily for both mother and daughter.

"It is miles in front of the common 'London success.'"—*Manchester Guardian*.

Cloth, 2s. net; Paper, 1s. net.

SIDGWICK & JACKSON LTD., 3 Adam Street, London, W.C.

SIDGWICK & JACKSON'S MODERN DRAMA

"Messrs. Sidgwick & Jackson are choosing their plays excellently."—*Saturday Review*.

THREE PLAYS BY GRANVILLE BARKER: "The Marrying of Ann Leete," "The Voysey Inheritance," and "Waste." In one vol., 5s. net; singly, cloth, 2s. net; paper wrappers, 1s. 6d. net.
[Fourth Impression.

THE MADRAS HOUSE. A Comedy in Four Acts. By GRANVILLE BARKER. Crown 8vo, cloth, 2s. net; paper wrappers, 1s. 6d. net. *[Fourth Impression.*

ANATOL. A Sequence of Dialogues. By ARTHUR SCHNITZLER. Paraphrased for the English Stage by GRANVILLE BARKER. Crown 8vo, cloth, 2s. net; paper wrappers, 1s. 6d. net. *[Third Impression.*

PRUNELLA; or, Love in a Dutch Garden. By LAURENCE HOUSMAN and GRANVILLE BARKER. With a Frontispiece and Music to "Pierrot's Serenade," by JOSEPH MOORAT. Fcap. 4to, 5s. net. Theatre Edition, crown 8vo, wrappers, 1s. net. *[Ninth Impression.*

CHAINS. A Play in Four Acts. By ELIZABETH BAKER. Crown 8vo, cloth, 1s. 6d. net; paper wrappers, 1s. net.
[Third Impression.

RUTHERFORD & SON. By GITHA SOWERBY. Crown 8vo, cloth, 2s. 6d. net; paper, 1s. 6d. net.
[Second Impression.

HINDLE WAKES. A Play in Four Acts. By STANLEY HOUGHTON. Cloth, 2s. net; paper, 1s. 6d. net.
[Sixth Impression.

MARY BROOME. By ALLAN MONKHOUSE. Cloth, 2s. net; paper, 1s. 6d. net. *[Second Impression.*

THE TRIAL OF JEANNE D'ARC. A Play in Four Acts. By EDWARD GARNETT. Crown 8vo, cloth, 3s. 6d. net.

PAINS AND PENALTIES. By LAURENCE HOUSMAN. Crown 8vo, cloth, 3s. 6d. net; paper, 1s. 6d. net.

ETC., ETC., ETC.

SIDGWICK & JACKSON LTD., 3 Adam Street, London, W.C.